# Once Upon a Group

*by the same author*

**A Practical Guide for Working with Reluctant Clients in Health and Social Care**
*Maggie Kindred*
*Illustrated by Cath Kindred*
ISBN 978 1 84905 102 6

*of related interest*

**Effective Communication**
**A Workbook for Social Care Workers**
*Suzan Collins*
ISBN 978 1 84310 927 3
*Knowledge and Skills for Social Care Workers Series*

**Working with Young Women**
**Activities for Exploring Personal, Social and Emotional Issues**
**2nd edition**
*Vanessa Rogers*
ISBN 978 1 84905 095 1

**Working with Young Men**
**Activities for Exploring Personal, Social and Emotional Issues**
**2nd edition**
*Vanessa Rogers*
ISBN 978 1 84905 101 9

**Helping Adolescents and Adults to Build Self-Esteem**
**A Photocopiable Resource Book**
*Deborah M. Plummer*
ISBN 978 1 84310 185 7

# Once Upon a Group

## A Guide to Running and Participating in Successful Groups

Maggie Kindred and Michael Kindred

*Illustrated by Michael Kindred*

Jessica Kingsley *Publishers*
London and Philadelphia

First published in 1984 by Southwell Diocesan Education Committee
Revised edition published in 1987 by Michael Kindred
Revised edition published in 1998 by 4M Publications

This second edition published in 2011
by Jessica Kingsley Publishers
116 Pentonville Road
London N1 9JB, UK
and
400 Market Street, Suite 400
Philadelphia, PA 19106, USA

*www.jkp.com*

**Library of Congress Cataloging in Publication Data**
Kindred, Maggie, 1940-
Once upon a group : running and participating in successful groups / Maggie
Kindred and Michael Kindred ; illustrated by Michael Kindred. -- 2nd ed.
p. cm.
Includes bibliographical references.
ISBN 978-1-84905-166-8 (alk. paper)
1. Small groups. 2. Social interaction. I. Kindred, Michael, 1937- II. Title.
HM736.K56 2011
302.3'4--dc22
        2010025986
**British Library Cataloguing in Publication Data**
A CIP catalogue record for this book is available from the British Library

ISBN 978 1 84905 166 8

Printed and bound in Great Britain by
MPG Books Group

# Contents

# 1

## Introduction

This book is aimed at providing a light-hearted and amusing approach to a subject which can be quite heavy. We hope that it offers an easily digestible way of gaining insights into how groups tick, while at the same time helping to overcome some of the anxieties and doubts which can make people shy away from anything to do with groups and their workings. Just the mention of a few 'in words' and jargon concerning group behaviour can be enough to put some of us off for life!

What follows, then, is a brief outline of aspects of group life with annotated pin-person drawings. Remember that behind laughter there may be a grain of truth! Of course, drawings and words are no substitute for the only effective way of learning how groups tick, that is, by belonging to groups of different kinds, either as members or leaders, and by taking part in competently led courses on groupwork.

Have fun using this book. Take the issues raised seriously, but don't take yourself too seriously.

*Maggie and Michael Kindred*

# 2
# Applying This Book to Your Situation

**Your role in life and work groups**

*We are all on the journey...our starting and finishing posts are different*

Groups are a universal phenomenon. Whether you are reading this book as a worker, volunteer, house-person or student, you will be a member of several groups. However, the patterns, customs and acceptable content may differ widely in different cultures and races.

Groups are mini-cultures in themselves, and represent all the issues which are present in wider society. It is important, therefore, to try to address some of these issues. For instance, women can be passive in groups, whilst men can unconsciously take the lead. Group leaders should find ways of trying to raise members' awareness, for example by:

- not making eye contact mainly with men when starting, giving instructions, ending and during the group life generally

- ensuring that when people from black and other ethnic minority groups are present they are not turned to as 'experts' on race

- being responsible for the attention of group members to unconscious racism and other forms of prejudice

- not using language which assumes that everyone is heterosexual.

Throughout the material in this book we shall try to make specific points about these issues. The drawings are deliberately designed to represent men and women of all ages, genders, sexual preferences, states of physical ability, races and social classes. However, make sure you adapt the content for your user group, including people who use signing, textphones and Braille.

## Groupwork and professional standards

If you are looking to use the book for gaining professional qualifications in the helping professions, the material is particularly geared towards the following:

*National Occupational Standards for Social Work*
Unit 8
Work with groups to promote individual growth, development and independence.

*National Occupational Standards for Youth Work*
1.1.2
Enable young people to work effectively in groups.

*National Occupational Standards for Health and Social Care*
HSC323b
Work with groups to promote individual growth and development.

*NVQ Advice and Guidance*
Unit AG27
Facilitate learning in groups.

# 3

# Running a Group

## A note on leadership

This book is designed to be used by 'non-experts' in groupwork, as we believe that anyone can lead well if he or she has a sensitive manner and knows certain basic rules. We hope that the material leads to the following conclusion:

*Of a good leader, when his task is finished, his goal achieved, they say 'we did it ourselves'* (Lao-tse, in Jacques 1984, p.154).

## Laying the foundations

These include what are sometimes called ground rules, and like the foundation of a building they are fundamental to its continued existence. They are very basic – so how is it that they are often ignored? We think that behind such apparently obvious points lie some issues which are not at all simple! (See the checklist in the Appendix.)

# 4

# A Brief Look at Origins of Group Behaviour

**My first group**

my first group | my first group

The first group to which we all belong is some kind of family or care group.

The ways in which adults and a child, or children, get on together – or fail to get on together – affect each member of that group deeply. The ones likely to benefit or suffer most are the children.

The ties and tensions may or may not be more complex where one-parent families are concerned, where substitute parents are involved, or where a child is fostered or adopted.

Our experiences in this first basic unit will affect how we react and behave in groups to which we belong later in life.

Think about recent experiences in a group. Were you reacting or behaving or feeling:

- a bit like your mother, father or substitute parent used to in a similar situation?

- a bit like you used to as a child?

## When groups become large

*One day, my first group seemed too big*

Jealousy directly involves two or more other people. We feel that we want to be included in something which is going on between them, but we are at present excluded. In wanting to get 'in on the act', we may feel like getting rid of the unwanted person or persons in order to make it a cosy 'twosome'.

Envy involves people indirectly. Someone else has a possession, ability or attribute which we would like very much, and our feelings become out of proportion.

Think back to the times when you were jealous or envious in a group.

Did those feelings have their origins in your early family life?

## Size of groups

*Some groups may be too large for their purpose*

Some people are 'only ones'. Others were born into large families. Some people were the eldest, others were in the middle, some were the youngest. Whatever your position in the care group, you would have feelings about it, just as you would have feelings about new members arriving.

Any such increase would affect how things were done, how present members felt about the new member, and vice versa.

These past experiences may affect how you feel about the size of groups to which you belong now. Have you been in any groups where 'too many cooks spoiled the broth'?

On the other hand, have you ever wished there were 'many hands to make light work'?

## Number of relationships and size of groups

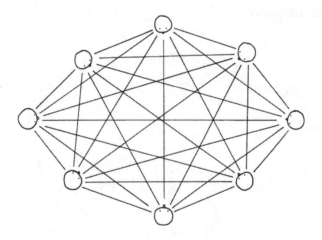

*In a group of only 8 people...there are 28 relationships going on at any given time!*

Part of the problem for a group which is too big for the job which it has set out to do, is that there are too many relationships going on for comfort. For example, in a family of carer, carer and child, the relationships which are going on are between:

- carer and carer
- one carer and child
- the other carer and child.

If another child joins the family, the number of relationships increase to those between:

- carer and carer
- one carer and older child
- one carer and younger child
- the other carer and older child
- the other carer and younger child
- older child and younger child.

Add *one* to a group of three and the number of relationships with which members have to deal has *doubled*!

Formula for working out how many relationships are going on:

$$\frac{(\text{Number in group}) \times (\text{number in group} - 1)}{2}$$

Therefore in a class of 30 children plus a leader, the number of relationships is $\frac{31 \times 30}{2} = 465$ (!)

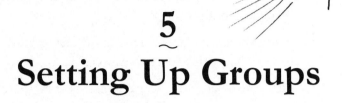

# 5
# Setting Up Groups

## Purpose and contract

*Members should be clear about the main purpose of the group...*

Think about various groups to which you have belonged. In each one did the leader:

- state clearly its purpose in the written or spoken invitation to join?

- give members the opportunity, at the first meeting, to say what their expectations were?

- offer the chance to see whether or not these expectations were realistic?

- discuss with members whether or not they understood the purpose of the group, and whether or not they agreed with it?

- make opportunities during the life of the group for evaluation of how the purpose was being fulfilled?

The more times you answer 'No' to the above, the higher the likelihood of genuine discontent in a group.

# Number of meetings

*Not everyone likes marathons...*

Have you ever been put off by the number of meetings planned for a group?

Perhaps you have gone to the first few sessions and then realized that a certain crispness is lacking, and that the task has been spread over far too long a time.

There is, of course, the other side of the coin. Have you sometimes felt that too much was being crammed into the time allotted?

The number of sessions planned for a group needs to be in keeping with the task to be accomplished.

## Meeting place

*Where and when you meet is important...*

Neutral territories are sometimes best. If you meet in one particular member's house all the time, you may find a few jealousies or resentments creeping in. It depends to a large extent on the members.

We imagine that you have been in groups which have gone badly in the most suitable of rooms. On the other hand, you have probably met in the most unwelcoming of places, and yet been thrilled by what happened in the group. However, what the meeting place is like usually matters more than people think. Warmth, comfort, acceptable lighting level and adequate space are all important.

Suitable access is crucial, including physical considerations such as the number of steps from the outside to the room. Think also about other kinds of accessibility: times when children need to be collected from school, and festival days for major religions. The timing can only be set with the specific members in mind.

## Seating arrangements – type of chair

*If possible, it's not a bad idea to have similar kinds of chairs for everybody…*

There are, of course, situations where this is difficult, such as when meeting in someone's home. It is important to realize that some people may need a chair of a certain kind due to difficulties such as backache or arthritis – this does not negate the 'similar chairs' principle.

If all the chairs are not the same, you need to be aware of how certain kinds of chairs can influence the contribution of the occupants. For example: someone who has cornered the only armchair, when everyone else is on hardback chairs, may use it to opt out of the proceedings quietly, or to feel superior, and to take a smug as well as a snug view of the proceedings. Someone on a stool may feel left out, and, literally, on edge!

The kind of chair used is important, although often it's Hobson's choice. One of us once went to a meeting held in a school for infants, where we were all sitting on incredibly small chairs for a very long time. It could have been described as an overflow meeting! No-one has perfect conditions. Telling people to bring a cushion has been an essential ingredient in 'joining instructions' for some courses.

## Seating arrangements – arranging the chairs

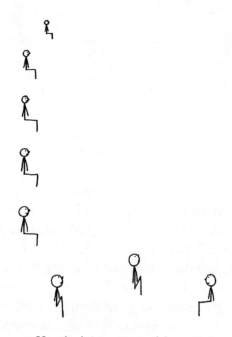

*How the chairs are arranged does matter!*

Have you been in small groups where the chairs were arranged so that you couldn't see everybody's face?

Have you been in larger groups and meetings where you could see mostly backs of necks?

In either case, how far did you feel part of what was happening?

How many times have you chosen to sit on the back row if you were not all that interested in going in the first place?

Holy (or unholy)
huddles can
frighten the life
out of someone
who likes
a bit of space
to themselves.

*In*

*particular,*

*don't*

*sit*

*on*

*top*

*of*

*each*

*other...*

## Physical and emotional space

*People need physical space as well as emotional space...*

Have you ever felt that you were sitting too close together in a group?

Or too far apart?

What is too close for you may not be close enough for someone else!

It is interesting to see the ways in which people knowingly or unknowingly adjust the space between themselves and those next to them.

Think about groups to which you have belonged. How would you have spaced the chairs?

## Size of meeting place

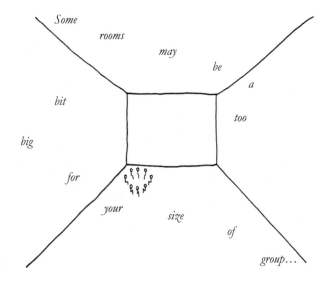

*Some rooms may be a bit too big for your size of group...*

Have you ever met as the only group in one corner of a large hall?

Some people can feel quite lost in that sort of situation.

Or have you suffered from claustrophobia and realized that feeling included has its limits?

The size of the place chosen for a meeting can affect the working of the group to some degree.

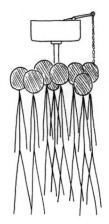

*...ontheotherhandtheycouldbetoosmall!*

~ 31 ~

## Temperature

*Getting the right temperature for the room is important …*
*it may also be difficult!*

The meeting place may be at an agreeable temperature at the beginning. But meetings warm up – physically as well as emotionally – as they proceed.

Have you ever been in groups where the leader checked occasionally that the room was at a comfortable temperature for everyone?

## Fresh air

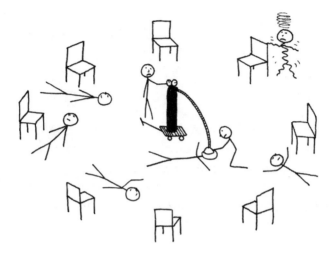

*There are other ways of getting some oxygen!*

Ventilating a room to suit all needs can sometimes be a problem. Some outdoor types would probably like to fling all the doors and windows wide open, while others may feel like fitting draught excluder strips during the coffee break.

A healthy stream of fresh air through an open window can turn one person's position into pneumonia corner. On the other hand the 'sealed capsule' syndrome may make some members feel stifled.

Perhaps you have welcomed those times where the leader 'aired' the problem, so to speak, and tried to help everyone to feel reasonably comfortable.

This point may seem laboured, but we believe that attention to basic physical needs symbolizes a concern for the less tangible needs and gives a powerful message that the leaders care about such things.

## Lighting

*Is the level of lighting more suited to interrogations or developing films?*

How often have you been in groups where the level of lighting has been given little consideration by the organizers or leaders?

It is something which deserves more attention than it usually gets.

One situation that can cause problems occurs when some members of the group are facing a window where bright light is coming through. They may find it difficult to engage with those members who are opposite them, who may think they are being ignored.

The level of lighting can create moods and atmospheres ranging from restful, to seductive, to dramatic, to intense. Our experiences in groups can be enhanced if we adjust the lighting to evoke the appropriate ambience.

## Breaks, including refreshments

*If you decide to have a coffee break…make sure it doesn't go on too long*

You have probably found it helpful when you have been offered one or more short breaks (depending on the length of the meeting).

Such breaks, one of which may include refreshments, give everyone a legitimate chance to stretch, yawn and change position as necessary.

Sitting on a hard chair for a long time can distract even the most interested and involved member.

Also the attention span of most people is less than we imagine. It is worth timing the breaks carefully: at the beginning a drink is welcoming but can postpone the getting down to work. Any break disrupts the flow. Some leaders wait for the 'right moment'. Others, ourselves included, feel this never comes, and that it is better to know in advance when the refreshments are going to arrive, and to organize the work around that timing.

# 6
~
# Boundaries
# and Rules

**Punctuality – at the beginning**

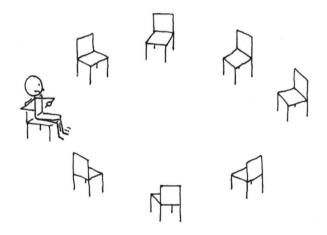

*It is helpful if the group starts on time...*

It can be frustrating, for those who have taken care to arrive on time, to wait for others who are late.

Some people are, of course, unavoidably late at times.

Therefore, it is important that groups and meetings start at the time stated, or else the number of latecomers is likely to increase, and dissatisfaction will grow among those who continue to be punctual.

However uncomfortable it may seem, it is generally better to welcome the late person by non-verbal communication and a brief word, than by attempting to recapitulate. This can more easily be done later.

Some people, realizing that they are late, may find it difficult to knock and enter. They are usually helped by knowing that they will get the kind of welcome mentioned above – thus they can come in with a minimum of fuss.

## Degree of familiarity

*How would you like people to refer to you in the group?*

Have you attended a group where you have been addressed in a way which made you feel slightly uncomfortable or embarrassed?

It is helpful for people to have the chance to say how they would like to be known.

Never shorten names because you find them difficult to pronounce. This applies particularly to unusual and 'non-English' names. Permission needs to be sought for the use of first names: don't assume this – check first.

## Commitment

*Groups work best if the membership is stable...*

If you say that you are going to join a group which is to have a series of meetings, it is important that you take this commitment seriously.

Nothing is more dispiriting to the leader and the regular members than spasmodic attendance.

There are some kinds of groups which, by their very nature, generate attendance which varies from meeting to meeting. Support groups and committees often fall into this category. The leader and members should take steps to use this kind of group as positively as possible, and therefore people should not be made to feel guilty about irregular attendance, but extra attention needs to be given each time to re-stating ground rules, introductions and endings. In this sort of group, each individual meeting covers the full range of group phenomena.

## Confidentiality

*It is important, at the start of a group, to discuss
the matter of confidentiality…*

The degree of confidentiality will vary according to the type of group.

A group which meets to help members with their personal problems will demand a very high degree of confidentiality.

Unless members feel that safeguard, how will they be able to share some of what is troubling them?

Some leaders fail to find an adequate consultant who is outside the group. They can then find themselves needing to talk to inappropriate people for support. It is amazing how such conversations return to their source, with unhelpful consequences.

Limits to confidentiality need to be stated, for example: 'If anyone in the group reveals that they have done serious harm to another person outside the group, which they have not shared until now, confidentiality cannot be absolute.' The group leader will consult with the person concerned and tell him or her what is to be passed on, and to whom. It is not the place of other group members to infringe confidentiality, but in extreme cases they cannot be compelled to keep silent. Fortunately, such cases are rare.

## Interruptions

*Sometimes there may be the odd interruption...*

Have you had experiences where the leader of a group has constantly broken off to answer the door or phone or deal with a family problem?

Did you feel that he or she was not really interested in the group and what it was doing?

The more committed everyone is will be in proportion to the productivity of the group. If someone leaves the room because of distress or a need for space, other members should follow *only* if it is considered that there is a serious risk to that person's well-being.

## Limits in general

*You may find it helpful to have a few boundaries and limits defined…*

These boundaries and limits apply to what people do in the group – what they do outside the group is their own affair.

A personal agenda is that which a person knowingly or unknowingly brings to a group, from his or her experiences outside the group. Sometimes people's personal agendas need to be looked at, as these can to a greater or lesser degree get in the way of what the group as a whole is supposed to be doing. We all have personal agendas, and with a little insight and help we can make sure that their effect on the life of the group is minimal.

If there seem to be particular personal agendas which are affecting the life of the group, there should be some encouragement from the leader for these to be acknowledged and discussed so that their effect on the group is minimized.

It is worth mentioning that, especially in discussion-type groups, some members will talk about anything but the subject in hand. Leaders can sometimes have a hard job in keeping them to the point. Those who have come to the meeting understanding its purpose, and are trying to fulfil it, may feel annoyed and frustrated.

## Smoking

*'Er…er…does anyone mind if I don't smoke?'*

The question of whether or not members may smoke should be dealt with in the publicity prior to the formation of the group, or at its first meeting. In public places, smoking must take place outside, but what about people's homes? Many buildings now have an automatic no smoking rule – it is becoming easier for private houses to follow suit, and for group leaders to suggest where people may take a 'smoke break' for example, in the garden.

Some non-smokers find it quite difficult to respond honestly to someone asking 'Do you mind if I smoke?' They may say 'no' in order to avoid having to cope with potentially uncomfortable feelings.

This can lead to suppressed resentment and can hinder the development of helpful relationships.

On the other hand, some smokers find it equally difficult to ask if they may smoke, knowing that some people don't like smoky atmospheres, and they too may sit through sessions with a growing resentment.

Either way, it is good to address the subject at the beginning.

## Punctuality – at the end

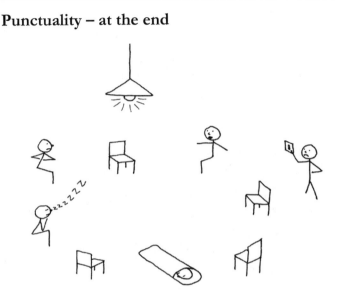

*It is helpful to finish sessions on time*

An important aspect of 'boundaries' is concerned with beginning and ending sessions.

Nothing is more annoying to most people than meetings which go on and on past their allotted finishing time. Some meetings don't even have a stated finishing time, and this can create difficulties for people who like to know how much time they are committing.

Finishing meetings on time helps to prevent boredom, fatigue, rebellions, walk-outs and reducing membership. Bringing up important issues at the last minute is a well-known phenomenon which can make meetings drag on beyond their allotted time (see p.94).

# 7
## Some Ways of Looking at Group Development

### Task versus maintenance

*Task versus maintenance*

Everything which takes place in a group is referred to as the 'process'.

This process comprises two distinct but interdependent functions: 'task' and 'maintenance'.

Maintenance is the building up and nurturing of the relationships between all members of the group.

If the task is concentrated upon at the expense of maintaining relationships in the group, then the co-operation necessary for the completing of the task will deteriorate, and so it will not be completed satisfactorily.

If the maintenance of relationships is concentrated upon at the expense of the task, the completion of the task may suffer setbacks, or may never be achieved.

Therefore it follows that task and maintenance need to go hand in hand, and although the degree to which either is attended to at any one time will vary, they should always be complementary to each other.

## Common threads running through various theories and models

There are various theories and models of how a group develops during its life. A brief outline follows of what seems fairly common to all these, showing that three basic phenomena tend to occur and recur.

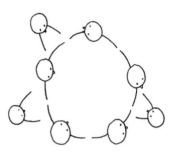

*A: 'Please let me in!'*

*B: 'The winner!'*

*C: Affection and disaffection*

At the beginning of the group life, members feel it is important to establish their position. The natural desire to feel needed and accepted and included is very prominent, although different members will show these desires in different ways.

At one or more points during the group life there will be bids for control, often directed at the designated leadership. Those doing the bidding will adopt different ways of trying to establish who is in control, varying from an open and frank attack on, or defence of, the designated leader, to more subtle ploys such as quietly manipulating others into liking the way they perform in the group!

As the group progresses, it enters its most creative phase. In the model we are using this stage is called 'affection'. It does not mean that people necessarily like each other, though this can be a helpful by-product.

These three phenomena are:

- needing to be accepted

- the desire for control

- developing confidence and commitment to the task.

They continue to appear in varying proportions during the life of a group, even though at different stages any one may seem more apparent than the other two.

## Creativity and play

*Some groups are more creative than others!*

What things give life to a group, invest it with a vital spark, make it tick? There are many, but one major factor is the degree of creativity among its members. This creativity is closely linked to the ability to play, which arises and develops in childhood – and very often is stifled later on by the stresses and pressures of adult life.

Think back to the world of the young. Children love to ask lots of questions, they are curious and want to experiment. They love to play not only with toys, but with odds and ends, and make things out of them. They have a rich fantasy life and a fertile imagination. They have a sense of wonder and delight in exploring the world around them. They have fun. This may describe the world of childhood for people who have either had a beneficial start in life, or who have experienced poor socio-economic conditions and ill health but have come through the challenges of the past in a positive way. They could be described as the 'fortunate' ones. The 'less fortunate' ones, who have experienced a difficult background that still affects them adversely, may have been deprived of many of these opportunities for creativity. Even so, in such circumstances, 'necessity is the mother of invention' may have been evident. It is also worth considering that 'fortunate' children may lose some opportunities for creativity by having ready-made toys and materials.

The more members of a group are in touch with the positive aspects of childhood outlined above, the more they will contribute to a group life which is lively and fun.

# 8
# What Goes On
# in Groups

**Choosing a seat**

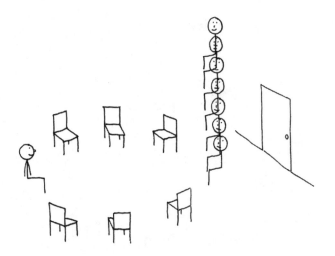

*Some people who are anxious about being in a group
may prefer the seat nearest the door*

If you are one of the first to walk into the room where the group is meeting, how do you choose your seat:

- next to the leader (if he or she is already seated)? Does this give you a feeling of kinship with the leader? Does it make you feel more secure and allay some of your anxieties?

- opposite the leader? Do you need to make sure you can see him or her? Are you preparing to do battle?

- nearest the door? Do you favour flight instead of fight? Do you need to leave early?

Do you find it difficult to take the last seat if everyone has arrived before you?

## Introducing a subject

*There are other ways of introducing a subject...*

How many times have you been in groups where the subject matter was introduced by a straight talk from notes? Perhaps you would have been more interested if one of the following had been used:

- slides and/or a tape

- role play – where members are given a particular situation and asked to act out how they would respond to it

- learning exercise – where members are asked to perform a particular task, and then helped to discuss how and what they had learned

- educational game – a game like Monopoly can be played and people are asked afterwards what criteria they used to make decisions, and how they felt about other players

- quiz

- passage from a book

- reaction to pictures and advertisements

- simulation – players enter into situations such as trading, setting up a workplace, producing a newspaper and so on, and discuss at the end how they reacted to other players, and to what was required of them during the simulation.

Be aware that many highly intelligent people have reading difficulties or are dyslexic. Make exercises tactile as well as based on words.

## Your opening contribution

*If you dive in with a big splash straight away, the leader may throw the odd lifebelt, but you have to learn to swim...*

Anxiety is largely responsible for the way in which some people make a contribution in the opening sessions of a group. They 'dive right in' and say things which they may regret later on. It is often difficult for them to go back on what they said – they are afraid of losing face.

Personality will also have some bearing on how and when we contribute to a group. For example, extroverts will be more likely to say the first thing that comes into their head. They will also be more likely to change their minds quickly in the light of new information, once again running the risk of diving in and creating a splash. Someone who is more introverted will tend to reflect on things before saying anything. Introverts, of course, run the risk of being considered uninterested or indecisive, and others may wonder what they are thinking. This is not to say that one way of contributing is right and another wrong – it is saying that it is helpful to be aware of how personality affects the ways in which people contribute to the group process.

A competent leader may be able to help 'divers' through the difficulties to some extent, but the person concerned has to take responsibility for the splash!

## Communication and lack of it

*People find different ways of not communicating with each other…*

Various things happen among the relationships within a group which cause breakdowns in communication.

The signs of these breakdowns vary from the very obvious to those which could go unnoticed.

Someone may deliberately ignore what another person is saying, and almost interrupt them, changing the subject at the same time.

Another person may be upset by what has just happened between themselves and another member, and avoid eye contact for the rest of the session.

Whatever the signs are, it is useful to be able to spot them, because we may be able to help someone who has borne the brunt of an 'exchange' and is feeling somewhat defeated, or hurt – or just plain angry.

## Non-verbal communication

*Sometimes, communication in a group may be of the non-verbal kind!*

Roughly 90 per cent of all face-to-face communication is non-verbal. If you would like to read up on this, see Wainwright's *Body Language* (2003).

We are so used to communicating by words, spoken or printed, that we sometimes forget that a great deal of what we communicate to others is done through:

- facial expression

- posture

- gestures (specific movements of fingers, hands and arms)

- skin (blushing, sweating)

- smiles and laughter

- crying.

It is sad that most of us are not very good at listening to what others are saying – we are usually more interested in what we want to say.

It is important to note that the same gesture may have one meaning in one culture and a different one in another. Think carefully before commenting on someone's gestures or posture. A simple example is the use of eye contact, which in some cultures means lack of respect or confrontation. So, looking down may denote respect rather than hesitancy or avoidance.

When it comes to being aware of the things which are not being put into words, most of us could do with developing such skills.

## Opting out

*Be sensitive to anyone who may be opting out almost unnoticed...*

Some people may become so anxious, threatened or frightened by what is happening in a group that they find ways of opting out.

They may remain unusually silent for long periods. They may even leave the room – this is often a cry for help or attention rather than a real wish to leave.

They may twist in their chair so as to try not to look at the group, or at a specific member of the group.

They may engage in 'pairing', that is, finding a mate in the group to whom they constantly refer for support, so that they feel safer.

They may make a lot of jokes about what is going on in an attempt to defuse a threatening situation.

A good leader will notice these signs and will try to help the person to feel a welcome part of the group again.

Silence, however, can mean thoughtful consideration. If there is a lot of silence, the leader should try asking what the quality of the silence is – this will open up the situation.

## Sensitivity

*Be sensitive to other people's feelings*

In your anxiety to cope with your own feelings, you may at times ride roughshod over other people's. Try to remember that every member of the group has his or her vulnerable areas, a tenderness which, once hurt, may take some time to heal.

So, what does it mean to be strong? Does it mean enforcing your will on others, keeping a stiff upper lip, bottling things up?

What does it mean to be weak? Does it mean sharing the fact that you are afraid of speaking in groups, that you are worried about being 'sat upon', that you find authority figures daunting?

What a lot of people count as strength is usually only a show of power used to cover up deeper insecurity.

What a lot of people count as weakness is frequently evidence of the humanity that we all share – how prone we are to make mistakes, to get things wrong, to fail to see what is in front of our noses! Admitting some of these things is normally a sign of strength and depth of character.

The paradox is that your strength may lie in behaving and reacting in a way which apparently strong people would dismiss as being weak!

## Honesty about feelings

*Some people are very honest when it comes to feelings –*
*other people's, of course!*

Try to imagine what you are about to say to someone in the group, being said by them to you.

How would you feel?

If you think you would feel all right, have you had more help than they may have had in developing insight into understanding oneself and others?

If you don't know, or aren't sure, then err on the safe side!

Start sentences with 'I think...', 'I feel...' and make sure that you don't speak for others. Asking everyone to do the same can be a very useful ground rule at the beginning. The leader will usually have to feed in a few reminders from time to time!

## The art of listening

*The art of listening may also apply to what is not being said...*

One of us once heard a child define 'listening' as 'wanting to hear'. There is an art to listening. It involves really wanting to hear what another person is saying. There is also an art to 'listening between the lines', to pick up what is not being said. Listening means more than just saying 'yes' and 'no' in the right places. Posture and gesture and facial expression can convey whether we are really listening or not. We are often so busy working out what we want to say that we wait impatiently for someone else to finish so that we can 'put our spoke in'. If you are not sure what someone is really saying, then use the counselling technique of checking: 'I think I heard you saying…is that what you meant?'

## Dominant behaviour

*Some people (only occasionally of course!) can be a trifle dominant…*

A person who is unsure of himself or herself, and feels insecure, may deal with these feelings in a variety of ways.

One way is to try to dominate others in order to feel less threatened by them and feel safer.

If a person is allowed to dominate the group, various things can happen: people will leave, the leader will lose co-operation from other members, the dominant person will take over the leadership, a rebellion may emerge when a few members of the group band together to 'sit on' the dominant one.

It is better if any tendency to dominate is dealt with when it is recognized.

It is helpful to deal with threatening emotions earlier rather than later.

The leader should work towards encouraging other members to help dominant personalities to take a back seat sometimes.

It is unhelpful for the leader continually to be acting as a controller while others enjoy the show and take no responsibility. He or she can pass the responsibility on by pointing out that the group seems to be expecting him or her to be a referee!

## Fight or flight

*Fight or flight (or freeze)?*

Most of us find it difficult to experience emotions and give ourselves time to decide whether or not we need to act upon them. Usually, the stronger the emotion, the greater the urge to act.

One example of this comes in what is generally referred to as the fight or flight response. It is very basic and necessary in the animal kingdom, and it is good that it is part of human nature too, but all too often it appears in inappropriately large doses in our relationships.

If someone in the group takes a tilt at us, do we rise up in anger and charge straight into battle, or do we turn on our heels and run like mad? Or are we rooted to the spot, frozen with fear?

Is either course really necessary if we think about it? Would it be possible to tell someone how their behaviour makes us feel, without acting upon those feelings? For example, would it be possible to tell another member of the group that they were making you feel like hitting them, and why this was so? In this way, you are at least offering the chance of opening up some kind of dialogue, which if taken can lead to a building-up of a relationship rather than a breaking down or abandoning of it. If the offer is declined, you are the one who has shown some insight and inner strength. It is always more helpful to describe how another's behaviour is making us feel, rather than condemning that behaviour. The rule about starting sentences with 'I' (see p.63) applies here.

## Democracy versus autocracy

*Some group leaders are occasionally less democratic than they might be...*

If a group leader comes over as rather autocratic at times, reactions from members will vary.

Some people enjoy being told what to do or think, and a relationship similar to that between a parent and child (appropriate enough in that setting) is maintained in an immature way between two adults, thus allowing little chance for personal growth.

Some people do not enjoy being told what to do or think, due to their previous life experiences. Rebellions against the leadership will almost surely develop.

Most of us fall somewhere between these two, and may find ourselves alternating in feelings about the leadership. This part of the 'control' dynamic is described on p.49.

## Bids for leadership

*Sometimes there may be a bid for the leadership...*

If someone has set himself or herself up as a leader, then you can be sure that someone else will want to knock them down.

If a group is meeting regularly over a period, the leadership may remain uncontested for a while (sometimes called the 'honeymoon period'), but after that, other people may begin to feel that they could do a better job.

A competent leader will recognize these bids, and bring them out into the open to be discussed and, hopefully, resolved.

If the bids are ignored, then trouble is in store, because members of the group will begin to take sides and the real purpose of the group will be in danger of being sidelined.

Once control issues have been resolved for a time, the group enters a creative period. It is normal for control issues to re-emerge towards the end.

## Co-leadership

*Co-leadership is not always easy!*

Have you been part of a group where, instead of just one leader, there have been two?

If they haven't spent a lot of time beforehand preparing how they are going to work with each other, and getting to know each other quite well, then the group will suffer.

For example, did noticeable differences of opinion emerge between them as to how the group should be run at different stages?

Did one co-leader try to wrench all the leadership for himself or herself? Did the other respond by doing battle, or by giving up and becoming to all intents and purposes an aggrieved member of the group?

Notice how co-leadership is handled if there is a man and woman team. Have the pair conformed to society's stereotypes, or have they made efforts to reverse these?

How is the whole group working on this? Do the women always make the refreshments, the men act as recorders and presenters, or are such tasks shared?

## Sub-groups

*Sub-groups can form...*

When two or three people begin to disagree with the leader, and with others who appear to be positive about the leadership, then the group will fail to remain a single unit working together for a purpose, and will become two separate groups within the group.

As with bids for the leadership, if this sub-grouping is not acknowledged and dealt with, the effectiveness of the group is at risk if it is a task centred group with a job to do. If the group is using the time specifically for studying itself, a simple 'mirror' comment about what is going on may be the best remedy, for example, 'I notice that there are several conversations going on at this point.'

Sub-groups tend to represent the wider society, for example, men and women, racial groups, gay and heterosexual people. At times, it can be useful to use these positively, like the women and men to work in separate sub-groups for a time. The support gained from this benefits the whole group when the results are shared.

## Pairing

*What is known as pairing can make people feel left out...*

If two people (or more) start sitting together at each session, and exchanging nods or winks, and whispering confidences, then this can irritate others or make them feel jealous and left out.

To make up for these feelings, other pairings can start.

The group is then on the way to disintegration in much the same way as when a sub-group has formed (see p.70).

The leader should bring the pairing out into the open and help members to look at the reasons for it, and the effect it is having on the group.

As a phenomenon, it may be a sign of insecurity, non-commitment to the group and its task, or the need to feel in control/be heard/have more influence. Check whether there are enough ways of ensuring that everyone's view is given equal weight. A useful device is a 'round'; that is, asking everyone in turn to state briefly their view or current feelings.

## Red herrings

*Red herrings*

At times, due to fear, enthusiasm, insecurity, rebelliousness, happiness and so on, most of us knowingly or unknowingly deflect other members of the group from the task in hand. Some people are more accomplished deflectors than others, but we all do it to some degree when we feel the need to change the subject quickly to avoid a 'hot potato' – we tell the story about what happened to someone outside the group, instead of what is happening to us right now.

The odd red herring here and there can be acceptable, especially if the group can be helped to see why such a deflection was used. A whole shoal unacknowledged could break the group net!

## Level of involvement

*Some people get too involved*

We all get involved in different ways and at different levels with any group to which we belong. The involvement can be practical, intellectual, emotional or spiritual – in any combination.

It will vary at different stages during the life of the group. Sometimes it will vary almost from minute to minute.

The reasons for getting involved are numerous – they include:

- interest

- excitement

- curiosity

- some emotional need not met outside the group

- pressure from one or more other members of the group

- some unrecognized need which is not being met.

It is difficult to say what getting too involved means – it will vary from person to person. An example of over-involvement which could lead to problems would be that of a group member continually wishing to focus on what he or she sees as other members' difficulties.

## Subversive behaviour

*There are those of us who can be quietly subversive...*

The rebellious toddler and the rebellious adolescent lurk in all of us!

When we take a tilt at authority or people we don't like, we can find it quite exciting and fun – it may not be so enjoyable for those on the receiving end.

Sometimes people will steer a course between being openly rebellious or 'awkward', and saying nothing, thereby probably bottling up their feelings. The subversion may emerge as a sort of 'borderline' remark where it is hard to decide whether they are being quietly rebellious, or whether they have put their finger on something important which is happening in the group which needs talking about.

It is worth noting that subversive behaviour can mask as constructive comment. Note carefully the kind of questions which are asked – are they a disguised way of catching the leader out?

Some groups or leaders may, of course, need to be challenged!

## Decision-making

*There may be odd times when it's difficult to reach a decision...*

Democracy has its advantages and disadvantages!

On the one hand it gives everyone a chance to influence the way the decision-making goes. On the other hand, it can lead to a watered-down form of what might have been a very creative idea.

In groups, it is important continually to evaluate the degree to which people feel free to contribute to the decision-making process. Is anyone feeling pushed out or ignored? Is anyone's opinion lightly dismissed without good reason? Is there a good level of co-operation in the group?

Note that truly consensual decision-making takes a long time. For some decisions, another approach may be better, for example, a sub-group of members who have some expertise works separately and brings recommendations to the whole group for ratification. A type of situation which needs autocratic decision-making occurs when a fire alarm goes off!

## Group norms

*'Please, sir'*

All groups, like families, have their own rules, often not stated, but nevertheless very powerful. These are known as the group norms.

Have you noticed, in groups to which you have belonged, what rules were being adhered to? Did the leader help members to be aware of what these were and try to ensure that individuals' rights were not being trampled upon?

A good exercise is to ask the group to write down what they think the unwritten rules are, once the group has had enough time together for these to evolve. You may gain some surprising insights into what is really going on!

## Barriers and defences

*Sometimes someone may erect the odd barrier...*

Life is a difficult business; in fact a psychiatrist friend once said that most people can't cope with too much reality.

So, right from birth, we put all sorts of emotional defences and barriers to help us cope with what makes us feel insecure, frightened, threatened, anxious, worried.

For example, perhaps you couldn't cope with your parents' anger, so now you tend to 'pour oil on troubled waters', and 'make the peace' in any situations involving confrontation, so that other people's anger is kept under, and so that your own doesn't surface. These defences are often described in a physical way like 'keeping a stiff upper lip' or having a 'poker face'.

Sometimes, the situation which has threatened us initially is repeated enough times for the defence to become a really hardened one. It can then get in the way of progress in relationships, so that someone can never allow natural feelings to show.

Contrary to popular opinion, competent leaders do not 'rush at people' to break them down. They recognize each individual's need for these barriers and try to find ways of making people more comfortable.

## Hidden agendas

*The hidden agenda…*

There are always things in people's lives outside the group which affect their contribution in the group. This is known as the hidden agenda. Sometimes it's not so hidden!

You take your emotional suitcase wherever you go. Some people keep their suitcases tightly locked, others let them spill all over the place. Most of us get a few things out from time to time, putting some back hastily – others the group may help us to wear for a time.

Things which have happened to us an hour ago, that day, that week, five years ago, in childhood, or things which are in the future such as a wedding, holidays, a difficult meeting, and so on, can be on our minds while the set agenda for the session is being worked through.

Some of these experiences may be positive, but some will have been upsetting enough to get in the way of our effective contribution to the work of the group.

That's not a criticism implying that we shouldn't let them get in the way – it is saying that we should acknowledge that this is normal for all of us, and should be recognized as such.

## Hanging bits of ourselves on others

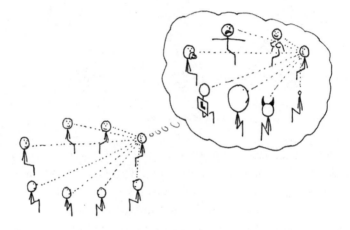

*How do we see other members of the group?*
*We may project aspects of our personality onto them...*

If I am 'big-headed' but am not aware of it, I can easily think of someone else as big-headed. I then don't have to consider whether I may have the fault of which I accuse others.

If I know that I have a cruel streak in me, and I wish that I hadn't, and don't want people to know, it is easy for me to accuse other people of being cruel. It lets me off the hook. It makes my own cruel streak seem not so bad if others are cruel too.

These kinds of 'projections' of aspects of our personality onto others, go on in different degrees all the time in any group.

Of course, it may be the other way round. In a group we may be under pressure to accept too readily others' views of us. The leader needs to watch for members' discomfort if this seems to be happening, as unreservedly taking in everything which people say about us is unhelpful.

If projections and the feelings associated with them are gradually acknowledged, and people make a genuine attempt to understand them, then relationships can improve. If unacknowledged, relationships will continue at a shallow level and any work the group has to do will suffer accordingly.

## The transfer system!

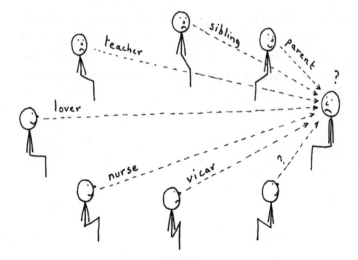

*Anyone may transfer feelings associated with someone they know outside the group to another member...*

This can be confusing, as lots of transferences can be taking place at any given moment.

Someone in the group may see you as the 'spitting image' of someone they know. Or you may have a particular characteristic, mannerism or type of voice which reminds them very much of someone they know (or knew).

If the person they are reminded of is or was 'lovely', 'fatherly/motherly' or 'very kind' in their eyes, you may find they are seeing the same qualities in you. If the person they are reminded of is or was someone they 'couldn't stand at any price', you may find that you are being ostracized by them, and it's no fault of yours.

The most common 'transference' concerns a person's parent(s). If, for example, a person really loved their mother, and you remind them very much of their mother, you may find them more than usually affectionate towards you. The reverse is also true. Many transference phenomena in groups come from experience in school – we have all spent a large part of our vulnerable years there. A simple exercise which helps people to discuss 'past experiences in groups' can be worthwhile.

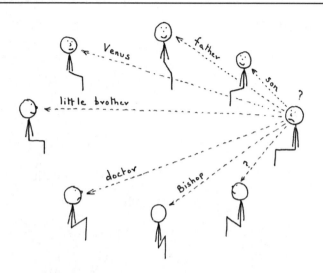

*What feelings associated with people outside the group are you transferring to other members in the group?*

If people are transferring things to you, what are you doing to them?

If you are afraid of a parent, for example, and someone in the group has an irritating mannerism just like your parent's, you may find yourself becoming afraid of that member of the group.

If these transferences can be acknowledged, there is a real chance that misunderstandings can be resolved to some extent, paving the way for deeper relationships within the group.

It can be quite helpful to become more aware of the qualities you put on to others which belong to significant people in your life, particularly parents.

## Scapegoats

*Why do we need someone to be the scapegoat?*

If you find challenges are entering into a relationship, or you feel that life is difficult at present, it is easier to blame other people or circumstances, than to take any responsibility yourself.

It is so easy to see the problems of life as being 'out there', and that the difficulties are caused by other people.

Of course, other people can cause us pain or anxiety and circumstances can be hard.

But that doesn't necessarily let us off the hook. We need to look at what part we are playing in a deteriorating relationship. Which problems are of our own making?

In groups, it is very easy to get another, perhaps apparently 'weaker' member of the group, to take the blame. They become the scapegoat for group problems which are not of their making, or may be only partly so.

*For safety, the scapegoat is sometimes located outside the group...*

Rather than find someone in the group to blame for the group's own shortcomings, it is much less threatening to blame someone or some 'body' outside the group. Likely candidates are:

- the system
- the management
- religious leaders
- the state
- society
- the government
- teachers
- doctors
- the youth of today
- God.

A competent leader will be aware of this 'running away' and will bring the focus of attention back into the group.

## The group casualty

*The group casualty!*

Have you found that sometimes one or two members of the group will initiate and encourage a 'case conference' about another member of the group who has shown some anxiety or fear or difficulty?

Soon, if the leader is not careful, everyone could become hooked on this golden opportunity to forget their own problems or the task of the group.

Have you ever come under the microscope in this way? If so, how did it feel?

Some may find the sudden attention flattering initially and join in the game eagerly. Eventually, the pace may hot up as the probes go deeper, and suddenly the 'patient' may be desperate to locate the exit sign. Others may immediately resent the appearance of 'doctors and nurses' who didn't seem to be there before. Either way, it is usually a harrowing experience for the one who is the centre of this kind of attention.

## Labelling and stereotyping

*Labelling people causes problems...*

A convenient way of addressing problems – our own and other people's – is to label and stereotype them.

If we can give a name to someone's upsetting or worrying behaviour, then it somehow seems safer; we may even be misled into thinking we have solved the matter.

It is much harder to avoid labelling people and instead treat them as fallible human beings like ourselves.

So, in groups, where feelings of insecurity can run quite high, labelling is an easy escape from trying to discover what is really hindering the growth of a relationship.

Labelling is particularly destructive in the use of language towards people from black and other ethnic minority groups, people with disability, gay and lesbian people, older people, and minority groups generally. The group needs to work out a way of trying to change language which may be construed as offensive.

## Point-scoring

*If you want to score points off each other ...*

If you are feeling somewhat at a disadvantage in a group for some reason, one way of trying to cope is to do or say something which puts another member (or members) at a disadvantage.

For example, someone may have disagreed with something you said. You then wait for a chance to disagree with them.

This game of 'point-scoring' can easily start in a group, and unless it is acknowledged and talked through, it can disrupt the real task of the group.

## Keeping on track

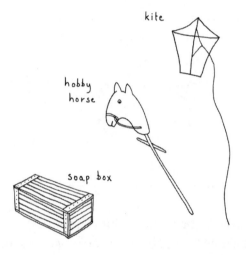

*Arrangements may have to be made for the disposal of distracting equipment which is cluttering up the group space...*

We all have our favourite topics, opinions about which we love to give other people benefit, 'pearls of wisdom' that people are just waiting to hear drop from our lips, and so on.

Irrespective of what the group is supposed to be doing, some people are itching to hold the floor and work the discussion round to themselves and their concerns.

They need to be steered, firmly and with kindness, back to the point. Again, 'rounds' (p.72) are a useful device to break this kind of pattern.

## Over-dependence

*Occasionally – well, quite often –*
*some group leaders can encourage over-dependence…*

We all need to be needed. This is normal.

Sometimes though, a person's need to be needed gets out of proportion because his or her needs are not being adequately met. So they strive to set up situations where their involvement is essential to people who are themselves in need.

Some social workers, doctors, ministers of religion, and people in the helping professions generally, fall into this category.

Some group leaders do too. This can mean that people in the group are not allowed to grow up emotionally. The leader, therefore, remains very much an immature source of wisdom, strength, help, comfort and so on.

A competent group leader allows members to grow in independence, including healthy disagreements and challenge.

## Silences

*It is important to experience silences (planned or not) –*
*however, some members may find them difficult...*

Unplanned awkward silences can be very threatening for some people, who may want desperately to do something to break the silence, but are afraid that if they do, all eyes will be upon them. Such silences may be the result of someone making a complaint or criticizing a member of the group, or have happened because the end of a topic has been reached and members need a time to reflect on what has been said.

The leader should not jump in immediately to end the silence, either by ignoring the moment or talking about it. He or she should wait a little while and then ask what the silence is about, so that it can be talked through.

Some people may also find that planned silences provoke anxiety, especially if they are long. Others can enjoy such silences together, and find them helpful and maybe moving.

So, silences, planned or not, can affect members differently.

Anxiety is usually lessened if people know how long a planned silence is going to be.

## Sexuality and sexual orientation

*The subjects of sex and sexual orientation are avoided…*

In a sense, this is quite right and proper in most groups. Unless the group's purpose is some form of either sex therapy or support for gay, lesbian and transsexual people, discussions about sexuality are probably an escape from the real agenda. Also, it would be 'beyond the pale' to discuss sex in groups in some cultures, and such diversity must be respected.

What is important is that *people* who are gay, lesbian and transsexual should not be made invisible, in the sense of assuming that 'There aren't any in this group'. How do members know that? Similarly, there are occasions of flirtatious non-verbal behaviour, which can be offensive.

The aware group leader or member is inclusive by his or her use of materials, as in the preparation checklist (see Appendix), and by not making assumptions that everyone is heterosexual. He or she will discourage any form of sexual behaviour in the group, including sexist jokes. Our essential 'maleness' or 'femaleness' is there for all to be aware of. It is our belief that we are all bi-sexual, so each male will display some female characteristics and each female will display some male characteristics. The good thing about groups is that they give people a chance to use some qualities that have lain dormant, such as the woman who becomes a little more assertive than before, or the man who allows himself to cry. These changes happen naturally by group members unconsciously copying others.

In these ways, groups can change attitudes and behaviour without anyone being embarrassed.

## Waiting until the last moment

*People often wait until the very last moment before saying what's really on their mind...*

It is well-known by counsellors and therapists that a client will often wait until the session has nearly ended before daring to raise a matter which is worrying them, or which they feel diffident about revealing. It's known in the trade as the 'door-knob syndrome'.

This approach is usually embarked upon because the client thinks that if any upsetting emotions are aroused by this late 'revelation', he or she can make a quick exit because time is up!

The same thing happens in groups and the situation needs careful handling. A leader could fall into the trap of beginning the meeting all over again, so to speak, in order to look at what has been raised and not appear dismissive. This could lead to annoyance among those who wish to leave on time. So, when this group phenomenon arises, the leader might suggest that the matter raised will be first on the agenda next time, as it needs to have the group's full attention.

# 9
# Endings

## Giving feedback

*Giving feedback…*

In some groups it may be appropriate for members to offer each other appraising comments to help develop their own performance. It is important, if such feedback is given, that the leader should define the rules for this and set an example. Feedback is helpful if it is:

- specific – 'When you mentioned X in the group on Friday I found it useful.'

- personal – 'When you keep interrupting Y I feel annoyed.'

Vague, impersonal statements which are not specific, such as 'Everyone in the group thinks Z is a waste of time', are unlikely to enhance communication among individual members or the life of the group.

Techniques such as asking each member in turn to state something appreciated or something regretted about the group may be useful. Another possibility is for each member to think of a symbolic present they would like to give each fellow participant. For example, someone who contributes many new ideas may be symbolically offered a computer. The presents can also provide a gentle form of feedback, so long as they are sensitively offered, for example, a telephone for someone who doesn't keep in touch.

## White elephants

*White elephants…*

Sometimes a person may reintroduce something which has previously arisen – they may even bring up the same thing repeatedly. Such 'white elephants' are particularly noticeable towards the end of the life of a group, and are a rather puzzling symptom of the ending process. With experience, group leaders are not put off by this as it is 'normal'. It can be helpful simply to point out to people that the particular subject has been discussed. If it hasn't, the group has some serious work to do! Although it is not usually possible in this life to resolve everything to one's total satisfaction, it is important to leave with a feeling that one has been listened to, and that concerns have been taken seriously. Otherwise, 'white elephants' turn into 'luggage' which can affect the next group.

Examples:

A may be seething at something B said five meetings ago.

C could be feeling hurt by a remark made by D last week.

E hasn't recovered from being made the group casualty two weeks ago.

F may feel that he or she just missed making a successful bid for the leadership. If only there were a few more meetings…

G may be cross with D for getting at C.

H may be the only one free of tangles and can't understand why people aren't enjoying themselves. (But if he or she can't understand, then it looks as though there is some unfinished business here as well!)

Remember that all endings replicate previous experiences of loss – this remains true even if the group interaction has not been experienced as particularly positive.

## Disbanding

*Some groups find it difficult to disband...*

Every group has a life of its own, and just as it was brought into being, so must it have an end.

Some groups, of course, meet for a continuing purpose and will go on year after year with changing membership.

Most groups, however, need a reasonable lifespan appropriate to their purpose. This avoids staleness, boredom and diminishing membership.

If people have formed good relationships during the life of the group, it is understandable that they won't want to break up. It is therefore essential that members have a chance to anticipate the coming feelings of loss, to share them, and to help each other in coming to terms with them. A party, games and small presents can help the process (like the symbolic ones on p.96 they should be sensitive).

## Celebrations!

*Celebrate success…*

This does not mean sweeping difficulties and unresolved issues under the carpet. It does mean making sure that the group's achievements are recognized. If the group has not already used some of the ending techniques suggested earlier, it will be particularly important to sum up what has been accomplished. A small amount of food and drink at this point is always helpful!

# Appendix – Running a Group Checklist

*Preparation for running a group is essential...*

Running a group may involve starting one from scratch or taking over an existing group. The checklist which follows relates to the former, but you can adapt it to the latter. For example, if you have been asked to take over an existing group, it would be wise to check that the purpose of the group is still clear to everyone, that the time and place of meetings are still convenient to members, and so on.

### What is the exact purpose of the group?

You need to make this quite clear to members.

Clarity is the key to success.

### When will the group meet?

Time, date and number of meetings.

Remember shift workers, people with children.

### Where will the group meet?

Don't forget TDP (Time, Date and Place) and number of meetings must go on any notices to prospective members.

### Is the meeting place accessible to all?

Are there any members with disability, either 'evident' – a person in a wheelchair, or 'hidden' – someone with a phobia about being on the upper floors of a high-rise building?

## What is the time contract to be?

Will you keep to time boundaries?

Starting and finishing on time will mean that members know what to expect, and those who have commitments at the end of a meeting, such as getting back to take a babysitter home, will not be inconvenienced.

## What arrangements will you make about confidentiality?

You need to agree with the members about what is for their ears only, and what may never be talked about outside the group. Unless this is established at the beginning and reinforced when necessary, members may be inhibited in what they say or do.

## What feedback will be allowed to people outside the group?

This is not the same as confidentiality. The group may at times be working on something which, for the time being, needs to be kept within the group, so that it can be worked out properly.

### Who will lead the group?

The person who does a lot of the preparation may not be the group leader and this needs to be clear to prospective members.

### Who will be responsible for which jobs?

There are some jobs which may not be the leader's responsibility, such as sending out notices and organizing refreshments.

### Will the meeting room be comfortable?

Consider temperature, ventilation, draughts, seating accommodation, lighting level.

### What about audibility?

Some rooms may be too big and have an echo. One person in ten has some degree of hearing impairment.

### If refreshments are to be served, what will they be?

Will food and drinks suit various cultures, customs and dietary needs?

## Is equipment in working order and are power points available?

Also check that CDs, DVDs, software and any other external devices will work on the equipment you will be using. There is no substitute for rehearsal.

## How will you handle lateness?

If anyone arrives late, it is better to continue with what the group is doing, rather than stop to bring a latecomer up to date, which can be frustrating for those who have arrived on time.

## How will you deal with smoking?

It takes only one person smoking to spoil the atmosphere for any number of non-smokers. It is worth putting on the notices which go out to prospective members that there will be no smoking allowed, or that the issue will be discussed at the first meeting to arrive at a mutually satisfactory solution.

Under new laws banning smoking in public places in some countries, there are NO SMOKING notices anyway.

## How will you cope with sporadic attendance?

Groups work best when membership is stable and committed. You may need to state on the notices which go out to prospective members that those who join the group are expected to commit themselves to full attendance, and that they are to let the group know when absence is unavoidable.

## Have you checked all materials?

Have you made sufficient copies of any handouts? Have you made a list of what materials you need for each meeting?

## Have you checked the 'messages' in your materials?

Do they give a positive view of people from black and other ethnic minority groups?

Do they convey the message that not everyone is slim, young and able-bodied?

Do they convey the message that there are gay and lesbian people as well as those who are heterosexual?

Do they convey messages which place women in an equal position with men?

## How will the ending of the group be marked?

The ending of a group is just as important as other parts of its life. Every ending is a loss, with feelings of loss. Rituals are important – see Chapter 9 for suggestions about giving feedback, disbanding and celebrating success.

# Bibliography

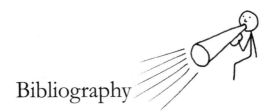

*Some groups can get too academic!*

We want to acknowledge here the indirect help we have received from those who have written about groups and their workings, as well as the direct help from the leaders of course workshops and seminars we have attended over the years.

We have made reference to:

Jacques, D. (1984) *Learning in Groups*. London: Croom Helm.
Wainwright, G. (2003) *Body Language*. London: Hodder.

## Further reading
Bion, W. (1990) *Experiences in Groups*. London: Routledge.
Brown, A. (1992) *Groupwork*. Aldershot: Ashgate.
Kindred, M. and Kindred, M. (1998) *Once Upon a Group Exercises*. Southwell: 4M Publications.
Maslow, A. (1984) *The Farther Reaches of Human Nature*. Harmondsworth: Penguin.
Schutz, W. (1958) *A 3 Dimensional Theory of Interpersonal Orientation*. New York: Holt, Rinehart and Winston.
Vernelle, B. (1994) *Understanding and Using Groups*. London: Whiting and Birch Ltd.